Spotlight on the
MAYA, AZTEC, and INCA CIVILIZATIONS

Ancient INCA GEOGRAPHY

Theresa Morlock

NEW YORK

Published in 2017 by The Rosen Publishing Group, Inc.
29 East 21st Street, New York, NY 10010

Editor: Sarah Machajewski

Photo Credits: Cover ostill/Shutterstock.com; p. 5 KasperKay/Shutterstock.com; p. 6 Shanti Hesse/Shutterstock.com; pp. 7, 15 https://commons.wikimedia.org/wiki/File:Inca_Empire.svg; p. 9 Toniflap/Shutterstock.com; p. 10 Aleh Mikalaichyk/Shutterstock.com; p. 11 MP cz/Shutterstock.com; p. 12 N. F. Photography/Shutterstock.com; p. 13 orangecrush/Shutterstock.com; p. 14 3523studio/Shutterstock.com; p. 17 Neale Cousland/Shutterstock.com; p. 18 courtesy of Metropolitan Museum of Art; p. 19 Ksenia Ragozina/Shutterstock.com; p. 20 Danita Delimont/Gallo Images/Getty Images; p. 21 Fotos593/Shutterstock.com; p. 23 rest/Shutterstock.com; p. 24 Aleksandra H. Kossowska/Shutterstock.com; p. 25 Glowimages/Getty Images; p. 27 Werner Forman/Universal Images Group/Getty Images; p. 29 Michael Fairchild/Photolibrary/Getty Images.

Library of Congress Cataloging-in-Publication Data

Names: Morlock, Theresa, author.
Title: Ancient Inca geography / Theresa Morlock.
Description: New York : PowerKids Press, 2016. | Series: Spotlight on the
  Maya, Aztec, and Inca civilizations | Includes index.
Identifiers: LCCN 2016002764 | ISBN 9781499419436 (pbk.) | ISBN 9781499419467 (library bound) | ISBN 9781499419443 (6 pack)
Subjects: LCSH: Peru--Historical geography--Juvenile literature. | Human
  geography--Peru--Juvenile literature. | Incas--Social life and
  customs--Juvenile literature. | Peru--Civilization--Indian
  influences--Juvenile literature.
Classification: LCC F3429 .M8417 2016 | DDC 985/.01--dc23
LC record available at http://lccn.loc.gov/2016002764

CPSIA Compliance Information: Batch #BS16PK: For further information contact Rosen Publishing, New York, New York at 1-800-237-9932.

CONTENTS

AN EXPANSIVE EMPIRE

Citizens of the Inca Empire lived in and around the Andes Mountains of modern-day Peru. The city of Cuzco was founded as the Inca capital around AD 1100. Beginning in the 1400s, the Incas built an empire that covered nearly 2,500 miles (4,023 km) along South America's Pacific coast. They did this by conquering neighboring peoples and taking control of their lands, citizens, and **resources**.

At its height, more than 12 million people lived in the Inca Empire. Rather than demanding resources from the conquered lands, the Inca required their citizens to contribute labor to public works projects. Together, under the direction of the government, the citizens of the Inca Empire helped each other survive in their harsh **environment**. In this way, the Incas created stores of extra food, **irrigation** systems, and their famous road system. Through studying the landscape of the Inca Empire, we can understand how geography affected the civilization's development. It determined everything, from where people lived to how they farmed and used natural resources.

The Andean people learned to live in their surroundings thousands of years before the Inca rose to power. How did they survive in this mountainous environment?

CLIMATE IN THE EMPIRE

The land the Inca inhabited included very distinct geographical environments—the Andean highlands, the Pacific coastal desert, and the western border of the Amazon rain forest. Each region is very different in terms of its climate and natural resources. Climate determined where settlements were made. Resources decided what type of farming and daily activities took place in a region.

When the Spanish **conquistadors** arrived in the Inca lands in the 16th century, the empire extended from the Pacific coast to the Andes Mountains, as pictured in the map below.

Generally, the climate in the Inca Empire was arid, or dry, in the West and **humid** in the East. Weather in some places in the mountains was cold and wet, but the lower mountain valleys had more temperate environments. It's here where most farms and homes were made. In the dry western regions, the Incas developed irrigation systems to bring water to their crops. The variety of geography in the empire meant that people in different regions could specialize in growing certain foods or creating certain goods.

THE HIGHLANDS AND THE FOOTHILLS

The Andes Mountains run along the western edge of South America. Cuzco, the Inca capital city, sits at an elevation of 11,152 feet (3,399 m). It was at the center of the Inca Empire. The northern mountain ranges of the Andes run in two parallel chains named the Cordillera Oriental and the Cordillera Occidental. Between the cordilleras is a high **plateau** called the Altiplano. This area is home to the fertile basin of Lake Titicaca. Lake Titicaca was **sacred** to the Inca.

On the eastern side of the Andes Mountains are the foothills, or lowland regions. Here, the mountains give way to the tropical temperatures of the Amazon rain forest. Although the Inca did not live in the rain forest, they harvested some plants that grew there, including coca plants. Coca leaves were popular for chewing.

> Aconcagua in Argentina is the highest mountain in the Andes—and in the entire Western Hemisphere!

MOUNTAIN ZONES

The Inca Empire occupied high peaks and low valleys. In some places, there is a height difference of 10,000 feet (3,048 m) between them! The geography can be divided into three general zones, and the weather and wildlife varies in each.

The three zones in the Andes Mountains are the puna, quechua, and yunga. The puna is the highest zone the Inca were able to use. It's located above 11,000 feet (3,352 m), and its climate is cold and wet. This area was good for raising some livestock and for growing crops that resisted the cold, such as potatoes.

A herd of llamas grazes on low-growing grasses in the puna zone.

The quechua zone, between about 7,000 and about 11,000 feet (2,133 and 3,352 m), has more moderate temperatures and rain. Here, Inca farmers grew maize (corn), beans, squash, and quinoa, which is a seed. Everything around 7,000 feet (2,133 m) and below is the yunga zone. It's warm and dry. Cactus plants and fruit trees grow well here.

The Inca raised crops that grew well where they lived. This protected farmers against losing their food to natural elements. They were able to trade for food that grew elsewhere.

THE PACIFIC COASTAL DESERT

Hardly any rain falls in South America's **unique** coastal region, no matter what the season. During winter, clouds formed by cold air moving over the Pacific Ocean are trapped beneath a layer of warm air from the high altitudes of the Andes. During summer, the upper layer of air cools, allowing the clouds to move over the Andes. This is where it rains.

The Pacific coastline is a dry place with few plants.

Traditional reed boats are still used on Lake Titicaca today.

Citizens of the Inca Empire who lived in the Pacific coastal region settled along rivers. The rivers provided freshwater. Fish and other kinds of seafood, such as shellfish, were the coastal region's main resources. Coastal fishermen used small boats made of bundles of reeds, called *balsas*. They caught their food with nets, spears, and copper fishhooks. Communities on the coast also grew crops such as gourds and cotton.

WHERE PEOPLE LIVED

The Incas called their empire Tawantinsuyu. In the Quechua language, Tawantinsuyu combines the words *tawantin*, meaning "a group of four," and *suyu*, meaning "region." In English, Tawantinsuyu roughly means "the realm of four parts." The Inca Empire was divided into four regions: Chinchaysuyu in the Northwest, Antisuyu in the Northeast, Contisuyu in the Southwest, and Collasuyu in the Southeast. Each of the regions had a unique landscape.

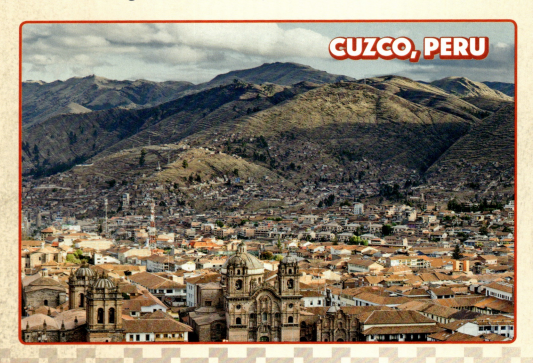

CUZCO, PERU

Cuzco, the capital of the Inca Empire, was in the center of the civilization's four distinct regions.

THE FOUR *SUYUS* OF THE INCA EMPIRE

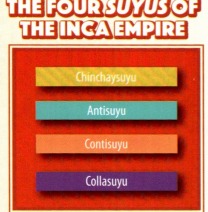

Chinchaysuyu

Antisuyu

Contisuyu

Collasuyu

SOUTH AMERICA

CUZCO

PACIFIC OCEAN

Chinchaysuyu started in the lowlands of the Pacific coast, extended through the Andes highlands, and ended at the edge of the eastern foothills. Antisuyu was much smaller, limited in size by the Amazon rain forest. The hot and dry Contisuyu was to the west, and its border touched the Pacific coast. Collasuyu was the largest of the four regions. It included the vast Altiplano and Lake Titicaca basin.

FARMING IN THE MOUNTAINS

The Inca people were accomplished farmers, yet steep mountains were a large part of their environment. How did they farm without naturally level land? They made it flat!

To overcome the challenges of farming in this kind of landscape, the Inca built **terraces** into the mountainsides. These terraces created level, usable land that was perfect for farming. The terraces were built like a set of steps on a mountain slope.

Terrace walls were made of stone. The walls kept the soil from being worn away by wind and other weather. The walls also soaked in sunlight during the day. This allowed the soil to stay warm at night, protecting plants from the cold. To make sure enough water was supplied to each terrace, the Incas built stone channels to irrigate their crops. However, the flat terraces also collected rainwater, which was helpful during periods of little rain.

> Imagine what this landscape would look like without terraces. The Andean people were able to turn steep, rocky mountain slopes into land for farming.

PREPARING FOR THE FUTURE

People living in the Inca Empire had to raise crops that could survive possible problems in their environment, such as droughts, or long periods of little rain. They also prepared for famines, or long periods of little food. The people made sure they had enough to eat by drying food to make it last longer. Farming tools included wooden spades, hoes, and digging sticks. They used bronze tools, too. Guano, or bird droppings, was used as fertilizer.

A bronze ax would've been helpful in battle, and possibly for farming and other daily tasks.

RUINS OF INGAPIRCA, AN INCA FORTRESS, IN ECUADOR

The Inca grew more food than they needed. They were allowed to keep a portion of what they grew. Another portion of their crops was given to the Sapa Inca, or emperor. He directed the government to keep the extra food in storehouses called *qollqa*. The stored food ensured no one in the empire went hungry. Finally, a portion of the food was given to priests to use during religious ceremonies.

RAISING LIVESTOCK

The Inca were skilled farmers, but they also raised herds of livestock for meat, wool, and transportation. Their animals may have also been raised as pets.

Llamas and alpacas were the most important animals to the Inca. Llamas could carry up to 100 pounds (45 kg) on their backs, and they could travel about 12 miles (19.3 km) a day. They provided wool and meat. Alpacas were raised for their wool, which was used to make clothing and fine **textiles**.

The Inca used these animals to carry supplies and transport goods throughout the empire. Llamas and alpacas **thrived** in the cooler highland regions, but not in the coastal territories—they only traveled there to deliver supplies.

The Inca raised livestock for practical reasons, but they were also used in religious ceremonies and feasts. The Inca also trapped wild vicuña, a llama-like animal, when they needed a finer-quality wool.

THE ROYAL HIGHWAY

The Inca transported food and supplies and communicated information across the large empire using a highway system. They named it Qhapaq Ñan, or the Royal Highway. The highway system spanned about 18,641 miles (30,000 km).

Instead of avoiding natural barriers, the Inca included them in the roads. They paved highland roads with stone, cut steps into existing rock, and constructed rope bridges from braided reeds and wood. The bridges allowed them to pass over mountainous **ravines**. The Inca didn't use wheels, so they traveled on foot and relied on pack animals to carry their goods.

The Inca roads were limited to government and military business. Common people needed special permission to travel on them. The roads were important because they connected the far reaches of the empire. Parts of the Royal Highway still exist today, proving that the Inca were experts at adapting structures to the existing geography.

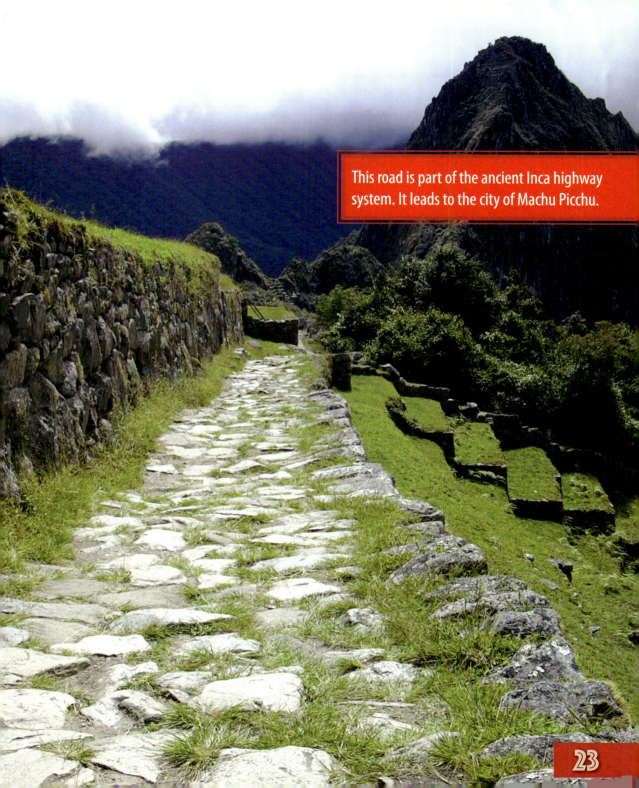

This road is part of the ancient Inca highway system. It leads to the city of Machu Picchu.

WORKING WITH STONE

The Inca were master stonemasons. A stonemason is a person who cuts and builds with stone. Inca stonemasons used granite, limestone, and andesite rocks to build their structures. These materials were readily available in their environment.

Through a process of pounding and grinding, masons shaped the large stones into blocks. Each block was then hauled with strong ropes over rolling logs to the construction site. There, the pieces were laid out on the ground in the right formation.

These are the architectural ruins of Choquequirao, an ancient Inca site in the Cuzco region. All the stones were shaped with simple tools and put together by hand.

The Inca used tools made of hematite and bronze to shape the stones. The rocks fit so perfectly together that they did not need mortar, or a binder, to keep them in place. To **buff** the walls and make them smooth, the stonemasons scrubbed the outer surfaces with a mixture of sand and water.

MINING PRECIOUS METALS

The Andes Mountains were rich with valuable metals, which the Inca used to make tools, weapons, sculptures, and jewelry. The Inca mined for copper and silver, but they were mostly known for their fascination with gold.

Inti, the powerful sun god, was very important to the Inca religion. Since the Inca associated gold with the sun, mountains that contained gold were seen as holy places. Offerings were made to the mountains and the metals they provided. Ceremonies were held in their honor.

Only nobles, the highest people in Inca society, had access to gold and silver. These metals were used to make jewelry and religious objects and to decorate the Sapa Inca's dwellings. Copper was used more commonly for jewelry and personal decoration. Bronze was used for making tools. Gold, silver, and copper were mined as **ore**. Gold was also collected through a process of panning in streams.

This gold and silver figurine was made during the time of the Inca Empire.

NATURE AND THE INCA RELIGION

The Inca people's relationship with the natural environment was the basis for their religion. Lake Titicaca was believed to be the site of the creation of the sun and the moon. The Incas believed that spirits lived in certain objects and places called huacas. Huacas could be rivers, caves, rock formations, or other sites. These places were considered sacred.

The Incas worshiped many gods, but the most important were Viracocha, the creator of the world; Inti, the sun god; Inti's wife, the moon goddess Mama Quilla; and Illapa, the thunder god. These gods were believed to control the weather, the success of crops, and the availability of natural resources such as gold.

The Sapa Inca was seen as the representative of Inti on Earth. Understanding how the Inca religion was tied to the physical landscape of the empire shows just how important nature was to the people.

At Ollantaytambo, Peru, a stone face overlooks the Inca ruins below. According to legend, it may be a sculpture of the Inca creator god, Viracocha, or one of his messengers. The ruins built on top of the face are said to be the figure's crown.

A LEGACY SURVIVES

The Inca Empire was very powerful from about 1438 to 1532—nearly 100 years. However, the empire collapsed quickly when the Spanish arrived in 1532. Under Francisco Pizarro, the Spanish captured and killed the Sapa Inca, conquered Cuzco, and kept the Inca people from rebelling. The Inca stood no chance against the guns and sicknesses the Spanish brought to their lands.

The Spanish changed the ways of life for the Andean people forever. However, the Inca's influence has survived. Descendants of the Inca people, as well as other cultural groups that live in the Andes, still use their traditional farming and crafting methods. Millions of Quechua-speaking people live in South America today. Most of all, the architectural remains of the Inca Empire are evidence that the Inca knew how to adapt to the unique environment in the Andes and beyond.

GLOSSARY

buff (BUFF): To polish.

conquistador (kahn-KEE-stuh-dohr): A Spanish conqueror of Mexico and Peru in the 16th century.

environment (ehn-VY-ruhn-munt): The natural surroundings for people, plants, and animals.

humid (HYOO-mihd): Marked by a high level of water vapor in the air, which produces a wet feeling.

irrigation (eer-uh-GAY-shun): A method of supplying water to crops.

ore (OR): A naturally occurring solid material from which metal and minerals are taken.

plateau (plaa-TOH): An area of high, level ground.

ravine (ruh-VEEN): A deep, narrow gorge with steep sides.

resource (REE-sohrs): A country's means of supporting itself, such as its land.

sacred (SAY-kruhd): Regarded with great respect because of its religious importance or connection with the gods.

terrace (TAIR-uhs): A flat area cut into a slope, often to provide farmland.

textile (TEHK-styl): Cloth, or a fiber used to make cloth.

thrive (THRYV): To live and grow successfully.

unique (yoo-NEEK): Belonging to one particular person or group.

INDEX

PRIMARY SOURCE LIST

Cover: Machu Picchu. Built by the Inca. Stone and earth. 15th–16th century. Located in the Andes Mountains, Peru.

Page 18: Axe. Created by the Inca. Bronze. 15th–16th century. Now kept at the Metropolitan Museum of Art, New York, NY.

Page 19: Ruins at Ingapirca. Built by the Inca. Stone. 15th–16th century. Located in Caniar Province, Ecuador.

Page 25: Ruins at Choquequirao. Built by the Inca. Stone. 15th–16th century. Located in Anta Province, Peru.

WEBSITES

Due to the changing nature of Internet links, PowerKids Press has developed an online list of websites related to the subject of this book. This site is updated regularly. Please use this link to access the list: www.powerkidslinks.com/soac/inge